D1512219

# Recipe for a
# good marriage

# Recipe for a good marriage

wise words and quirky advice for happy, long-lasting relationships

RYLAND
PETERS
& SMALL

LONDON NEW YORK

## Cheryl Saban

First published in the United States
in 2005 by Ryland Peters & Small
519 Broadway, 5th Floor
New York, NY 10012
www.rylandpeters.com

Designer Catherine Griffin
Commissioning editor Annabel Morgan
Picture research Emily Westlake
Production Sheila Smith
Art director Gabriella Le Grazie
Publishing director Alison Starling

10 9 8 7 6 5 4

ISBN 978-1-84172-786-8

Printed and bound in China.

# contents

*Recipe for a Good Marriage* is affectionately dedicated to lovers everywhere. This little tome is the result of the good wishes and quirky advice my girlfriends offered to my daughter on the occasion of her wedding shower. The cheeky tidbits of wisdom were lovingly gathered from married and unmarried women of all ages.

The common denominator among us appears to be the ubiquitous hope for lasting love, passion, and friendship with a mate. Some of the tips are laughable, some are a bit off-color, but for the most part they speak to the playful cupid in us all. This good-hearted guidance is sometimes silly, sometimes raunchy, but it is always based on experience.

I thank all of my delightful girlfriends for so willingly sharing their views on life. And no book on love recipes would be possible without my main ingredient, my husband, Haim. I send you a kiss, my love. You are my partner, my lover, my husband, and my friend—the one who cooks all of my love recipes to perfection. May we always be like chocolate for one another.

Marriage isn't
ownership.
It's a partnership.

LOVE ME WHEN I LEAST DESERVE IT,
BECAUSE THAT IS WHEN I REALLY NEED IT.
SWEDISH PROVERB

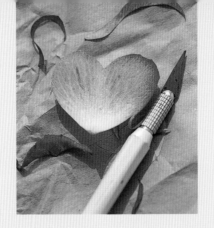

Love each other
unconditionally.

A GOOD HUSBAND MAKES A GOOD WIFE.

JOHN FLORIO (1533–1625), FROM "SECOND FRUITS"

Opposites might attract,
But it's our similarities
that keep us together.

LET THE HUSBAND RENDER UNTO
THE WIFE DUE BENEVOLENCE:
AND LIKEWISE ALSO THE WIFE
UNTO THE HUSBAND.

THE BIBLE, I CORINTHIANS 7:3

Agree to disagree.
You're individuals,
after all...
not clones.

THERE IS NO MORE LOVELY, FRIENDLY
AND CHARMING RELATIONSHIP,
COMMUNION OR COMPANY THAN
A GOOD MARRIAGE.

MARTIN LUTHER (1483–1546),
FROM "TABLE TALK"

Love

=

Passion

+

Friendship

+

Unconditional affection.

YOU WERE BORN TOGETHER, AND TOGETHER YOU
SHALL BE FOREVERMORE...
BUT LET THERE BE SPACES IN YOUR TOGETHERNESS,
AND LET THE WINDS OF THE HEAVENS DANCE BETWEEN YOU.
KAHLIL GIBRAN (1883–1931), FROM "THE PROPHET"

Learn to be tolerant
of your differences,
and respect them.

A GOOD MARRIAGE... IS A SWEET ASSOCIATION IN LIFE: FULL OF CONSTANCY, TRUST, AND AN INFINITE NUMBER OF USEFUL AND SOLID SERVICES AND MUTUAL OBLIGATIONS.
MICHEL DE MONTAIGNE (1533–1592), FROM "ON SOME VERSES OF VIRGIL"

Take care of each other.
Share secrets.
Create a private club
with just the two
of you in it.

THE SUPREME HAPPINESS IN LIFE
IS THE ASSURANCE OF BEING
LOVED FOR ONESELF,
EVEN IN SPITE OF ONESELF.

VICTOR HUGO (1802–1885),
FROM "LES MISÉRABLES"

Don't lose yourself.
Remember why you
got together in the
first place.

KINDNESS IN WOMEN, NOT THEIR BEAUTEOUS LOOKS,
SHALL WIN MY LOVE

**WILLIAM SHAKESPEARE (1564–1616), FROM "THE TAMING OF THE SHREW"**

Think twice before you
say something critical.
Hurt feelings can take a
long time to heal.

A GOOD MARRIAGE IS THAT IN WHICH EACH APPOINTS
THE OTHER GUARDIAN OF HIS SOLITUDE.

RAINER MARIA RILKE (1875–1926), FROM "LETTERS TO A YOUNG POET"

Keep a place both
physically and
spiritually for yourself.
Private time is
important.

*lovers*

Pretend you're still dating.
Prepare romantic dinners
together, and eat by candlelight.

# GIVE ALL TO LOVE.

RALPH WALDO EMERSON (1803–1882), FROM "POEMS"

Bring flowers to each
other... just because.
Small gestures can
make BIG impressions.

MAN AND WIFE, BEING
TWO, ARE ONE IN LOVE.
WILLIAM SHAKESPEARE
(1564–1616), FROM "HENRY V"

Have fun
Thrill each other
Naked dancing
Masks
Feathers
Dress up
Be silly
Make love!

LICENCE MY ROVING HANDS, AND LET THEM GO,
BEFORE, BEHIND, BETWEEN, ABOVE, BELOW.
JOHN DONNE (C. 1572–1631), FROM "TO HIS MISTRESS GOING TO BED"

Have breakfast in bed
for you and your man
on lazy Sundays.

COME LIVE WITH ME,
AND BE MY LOVE,
AND WE WILL SOME
NEW PLEASURES PROVE
OF GOLDEN SANDS,
AND CRYSTAL BROOKS,
WITH SILKEN LINES,
AND SILVER HOOKS.

JOHN DONNE (C. 1572–1631),
FROM "THE BAIT"

Find time for an occasional
weekend getaway.
Stepping outside your everyday
routine can add spice
to your life.

I MARRIED MY HUSBAND FOR LIFE,
NOT FOR LUNCH.

**ORIGIN UNKNOWN**

Care for your
love tenderly.
Love that is
nurtured can last
forever... and that's
a long, long time.

How do I love thee? Let me count the ways.
I love thee to the depth and breadth and
height my soul can reach.

**ELIZABETH BARRETT BROWNING (1806–1861),
FROM "SONNETS FROM THE PORTUGUESE"**

Remember to have date nights. Though we all have many obligations in life, take time regularly to be ALONE with each other.

MARRIAGE HAS MANY PAINS, BUT
CELIBACY HAS NO PLEASURES.

SAMUEL JOHNSON (1709–1784),
FROM "RASSELAS"

Candlelight...
Champagne...
Beautiful sheets...
Sex, Sex,
Sex!

WHEN LOVE HAS MELTED AND MINGLED TWO
BEINGS INTO AN ANGELIC AND SACRED UNITY,
THE SECRET OF LIFE IS FOUND FOR THEM…
THEY ARE THEN BUT THE TWO WINGS OF A
SINGLE SPIRIT. LOVE, SOAR!

VICTOR HUGO (1802–1885), FROM "LES MISÉRABLES"

Take romantic
vacations often, and
bring sexy lingerie.

*friends*

Communicate!
Communicate!
Communicate!

MATRIMONY IS THE HIGH SEA
FOR WHICH NO COMPASS HAS
YET BEEN INVENTED.
HEINRICH HEINE (1797–1856)

Pick fights carefully.
Unless it's
worth a divorce,
GIVE IT UP.
Life is too short.

BE TO THEIR VIRTUE VERY KIND;
BE TO THEIR FAULTS A LITTLE BLIND.
MATTHEW PRIOR (1664–1721), FROM "AN ENGLISH PADLOCK"

Don't take anything too seriously, and keep talking! The "silent treatment" doesn't work.

THE QUALITY OF A MARRIAGE
IS PROVEN BY ITS ABILITY TO
TOLERATE AN OCCASIONAL
"EXCEPTION."

**FRIEDRICH NIETZSCHE (1844–1900),
FROM "TEST OF A GOOD MARRIAGE"**

Never go to bed angry...
Stay up all night
and fight!

OF ALL SERIOUS THINGS, MARRIAGE IS THE FUNNIEST.

PIERRE DE BEAUMARCHAIS (1732–1799), FROM "THE MARRIAGE OF FIGARO"

Work on your
sense of humor.
You are going to
NEED it!

THE BEST FRIEND WILL PROBABLY GET THE
BEST SPOUSE, BECAUSE A GOOD MARRIAGE
IS BASED ON THE TALENT FOR FRIENDSHIP.
**FRIEDRICH NIETZSCHE (1844–1900), FROM "FRIENDSHIP AND MARRIAGE"**

Be willing to
communicate,
and then
negotiate.

MARRIAGE IS THE HIGHEST STATE OF FRIENDSHIP:
IF HAPPY, IT LESSENS OUR CARES BY DIVIDING
THEM, AT THE SAME TIME THAT IT DOUBLES OUR
PLEASURES BY MUTUAL PARTICIPATION.
SAMUEL RICHARDSON (1689–1761), FROM "CLARISSA"

Make love,
connect,
talk,
respect,
and stand
by your man...
and expect him
to stand by you.

KEEP YOUR EYES WIDE
OPEN BEFORE MARRIAGE,
HALF SHUT AFTERWARDS.
BENJAMIN FRANKLIN
(1706–1790), FROM
"POOR RICHARD'S ALMANAC"

Ignore
EVERYTHING
petty,
and smile!

IN MARRIAGE DO THOU BE WISE;
PREFER THE PERSON BEFORE MONEY;
VIRTUE BEFORE BEAUTY;
THE MIND BEFORE THE BODY.
WILLIAM PENN (1644–1718), FROM "SOME FRUITS OF SOLITUDE"

Say
"I love you"
every day.

# picture credits

Polly Wreford: endpapers, pages 1–3, 17, 20, 25 inset, 27, 30, 32, 42, 50, 52, 53, 55, 58;
Caroline Arber: pages 13, 22, 26, 31 inset, 39, 46–47, 48, 54;
Dan Duchars: pages 8–9, 16, 21 background, 31 background, 51 inset, 56;
Debi Treloar: pages 14, 40, 43 inset, 45, 49, 51 background, 62;
David Brittain: pages 15 background, 19, 28–29, 57 inset, 61;
Daniel Farmer: pages 5, 25 background, 44, 57 background, 60;
Peter Cassidy: pages 34, 35, 43 background; James Merrell: pages 4, 11, 18;
Chris Tubbs: pages 36, 37 background; Jan Baldwin: pages 15 inset, 37 inset;
Sandra Lane: pages 23, 24; David Montgomery: pages 6, 38;
Carolyn Barber: page 63; Martin Brigdale: page 7;
Catherine Gratwicke: page 21 inset; Emma Lee: page 10; Andrew Wood: page 12.

Items on pages 39 & 46–47 designed by Caroline Zoob (00 44 1273 479274)